ABOUT DARTMO[...]

First published in Great Br[...]

Copyright © Trevor James

ISBN 1 898964 46 7

Orchard Publications
2 Orchard Close, Chudleigh, Newton Abbot, Devon TQ13 0LR
Telephone: (01626) 852714

Printed by
Hedgerow Print, Crediton, Devon EX17 1ES

ACKNOWLEDGEMENTS

The contents of this little book have been gathered over a period of several years with the kind help of friends and colleagues in the Prison Service, Officers of Devon and Cornwall Constabulary and various public bodies in Plymouth and Exeter. Other friends have been more than generous with advice and photographs. The author expresses his gratitude to them all.

Special thanks are due to: Mr. John Lawrence, former Governor of Dartmoor Prison, who kindly granted facilities and assisted in other ways; Prison Officer Mike Chamberlain who shared his abundant knowledge of the prison so freely; P.C. Simon Dell, M.B.E., of Tavistock for his cheerful encouragement and for supplying some of the illustrations.

This appraisal of Dartmoor Prison's history is respectfully dedicated to Prison Officers everywhere, who do an often difficult job as custodians of Britain's criminals, and to the Police Forces who track them down and bring them to justice.

Prison Officer Dog Handler Mick Smith and German Shepherd Dog Oscar.
Dogs live with their handlers and a strong bond of loyalty and affection exists beween them.

ABOUT DARTMOOR PRISON

CONTENTS

PREFACE

This brief account of Dartmoor Prison's turbulent past may surprise visitors to Princetown curious about Britain's most famous jail. It was built for French prisoners of war, not by them – contractors tendered for the work and employed local labour. Many people do not realise Dartmoor held American prisoners too, captured during the War of 1812 (a glance at the date will also correct the notion that it was the War of Independence). The French and American prisoners of war built the Church of St. Michael and All Angels at Princetown, which makes it unique in all of Britain.

The full story of Dartmoor prison has yet to be written. Its history is long and complicated, encompassing the tempestuous years of the War Depot, and the later phase when convicts suffered under a merciless regime, often for 'crimes' which would barely warrant a custodial sentence now. History in general is neither 'romantic' or 'colourful', nor is the story of Dartmoor Prison. The prison system which drove some men mad and others to suicide, must be a lesson to us all – that persecution for its own sake is not the answer to crime prevention.

Prison block and boundary wall. The chimneys are associated with the old warm air heating system and are now obsolete.

INTRODUCTION

The prison was built between 1805 and 1809 at the instigation of Sir Thomas Tyrwhitt, Lord Warden of the Stannaries and founder of Prince's Town as it was first called.

Sir Thomas was a close friend of the Prince of Wales, the future Prince Regent and King George IV. As the Sovereign's eldest son, the Prince also held the title Duke of Cornwall and, like our present heir to the throne, received the income from the Duchy of Cornwall until he became King. Much of Dartmoor, including Princetown, forms part of the Duchy Estates and it was in 1785, as the Prince's Private Secretary, that Sir Thomas first came to the area (he was plain 'Mr.' Tyrwhitt then, being Knighted in 1812 prior to his appointment as Usher to Black Rod). Like others before him he thought there was a potential for creating an agricultural farming community on the moor and he leased 2,500 acres from the Duchy for that purpose. He built a country home and estate, which he named 'Tor Royal', not far from the ancient track that crossed the moor from Plymouth to what is now Two Bridges.

Sir Thomas Tyrwhitt's efforts farming on Dartmoor were unsuccessful. The climate and the soil are not suitable for growing crops without massive injections of fertiliser and an abundance of labour and to this day farming on the high moor is limited to grazing sheep and cattle. By the turn of the century his ambitious plans for cultivating the moor and populating the area with new settlers were in decline. Princetown would probably not have amounted to more than a wayside hamlet but for the resumption of the war with France in 1803. The Treaty of Amiens (1802–1803) had proved unreliable and when the French appeared to be planning an invasion, Britain once again declared war. It lasted eleven years and was to affect the little Dartmoor town in an unexpected manner.

From the very beginning of the war the Royal Navy literally 'ruled the waves', blockading French ports, intercepting and capturing their vessels (many of them privateers) and taking many thousands of prisoners. Soon the old war prisons at Stapleton (Bristol), Normans Cross (Peterborough) and Mill Prison (Plymouth), were full and overcrowded. To help alleviate the situation the notorious 'hulks' were brought into use. These were redundant Ships of the Line, many of which had for years been rotting at anchor in secluded creeks all around the coasts of Britain.

Responsibility for prisoners of war lay with the Board of Transport, known simply as the 'Transport Office', a government department which came under the jurisdiction of the British Admiralty. In June 1805 approval was sought from their Lordships at the Admiralty for a shore depot to be built in the County of Devon, capable of accommodating 5,000 prisoners of war. Conditions on the hulks were appalling. The meagre rations, poor sanitary arrangements, the reeking atmosphere below decks and lack of exercise, caused the death rate to rise to an unacceptable level. Another important consideration was the reduction in expenditure: the annual cost of running the prison was an estimated £3,000 compared to at least £18,000 for the six prison ships at Plymouth. Sir Thomas Tyrwhitt, who by this time held a number of appointments, including Lord Warden of the Stannaries, Member of Parliament for Portarlington and Vice Admiral of Devon and Cornwall, realised this was a chance to develop Princetown if only the authorities could be convinced it was the most appropriate location for a war prison. There can be no doubt he influenced the decision to build the prison adjacent to the little settlement that was named by him in honour of his lifelong friend and mentor, His Royal Highness the Prince of Wales.

French prisoners of war marching to Dartmoor Depot under escort.
From a painting by an unknown prisoner at Dartmoor Prison.

DARTMOOR DEPOT

On 29th March 1806 Sir Thomas Tyrwhitt laid the foundation stone for Dartmoor Depot, as it was first called. The site seemed ideal: it was far enough away from Plymouth and the Dartmoor towns for security, yet close enough to rush reinforcements there should the need arise. Plenty of 'moorstone' (the natural stones that lie scattered all over Dartmoor) was available and there was an abundance of granite in the nearby quarries. One of the most important requirements was water, obtained by constructing a leat (shallow watercourse) from the River Walkham to a reservoir adjacent to the prison (the little tower from which the water was released to flow by gravity to the prison blocks can still be seen opposite the main prison entrance). Finally, the Prince of Wales agreed to lease the quantity of land required (Dartmoor prison still pays an annual rent to the Duchy).

There were drawbacks however. It was an isolated spot 1400 ft. above sea level, exposed to the worst of Dartmoor storms and blazing summer heat and accessible only by roads often rendered impassable by flood or snow in winter. Masons and labourers were recruited from as far away as Penryn and Falmouth in Cornwall. Many of these men walked there looking for employment, only to return home soon afterwards because of the low wages and hardships working on the open moor. Consequently, the construction work took nearly twice as long as anticipated and cost almost double the estimate submitted by Messrs. Isbell Rowe and Company, the successful Plymouth contractor. The actual figures were:

Mr. Daniel Alexander's (Architect) original estimate
to the Transport office £70,146
The successful contractor, Isbell Rowe and Company,
who submitted the lowest estimate of £66,815
Actual final cost £135,000

When the first prisoners arrived on 24th May 1809 building work was still in progress and some of it was of such poor quality it had to be done again. All the same it was a huge undertaking and a spectacular one. When it was finished a stone fortress had arisen on a barren moor, surrounded by a high wall that enclosed more than fifteen acres, with a separate barracks for the 500 officers and men, mainly Militiamen, who were to guard it (their numbers eventually exceeded 1200 as the number of prisoners rose).

THE PRISON

This is what the prison looked like on completion. Two high circular walls, nearly a mile in circumference, enclosed five prison blocks, a hospital and a separate prison for the officers. The gap between the walls was called the 'Military Walk' and it was from there the sentries had access to wooden platforms mounted on the inner wall, enabling them to keep watch on the interior. The stone-built prison blocks were three stories high, with slate roofs and concrete floors, except for the top floor which had timber flooring and was originally intended to be an exercise area in bad weather. Each of the first two floors were open dormitories, with rows of iron posts from which the prisoners could sling their hammocks, 500 of them to each floor. There were no heating arrangements and the two-foot square 'windows' were unglazed. Here men lived together for years, eating, sleeping, fighting, gambling (and often dying) in such close proximity to each other their bodily heat alone kept them alive in the winter months, when the cold froze their breath in layers on the walls. As more prisoners arrived all three floors had to be used to accommodate them and 1,500 men were crammed into prison blocks intended for 1,000. In 1811 two more blocks were built and quickly filled as the number of prisoners rose to nearly 10,000. The work was done by French prisoner volunteers who were paid for their labour, not forcibly employed (this could explain how the myth about them building the prison itself originated).

The prisons occupied the lower half of the interior, hemmed in by the military walks and a stone wall that shut them off from the upper portion. In the other half of the prison, to the left of the main entrance, was the hospital, manned by a Surgeon of the Royal Navy assisted by nurses and washermen recruited from the prisoners. They were paid sixpence a day for their services and got first share of the clothes of those who died. The corpses were examined to ascertain and record the cause of death, after which they were stripped of their clothing and removed to the 'Dead House' beyond the boundary walls to await burial.

Opposite the hospital was the 'Petty Officer's Prison' where officer prisoners lived. Most officers had the chance to live 'on parole' as free men in the neighbouring towns, on condition they gave their word of honour not to escape and to obey the parole rules. Several hundred did escape however and those who were recaptured, together with officers who flaunted the rules, were sent to the war prisons where they joined those who refused parole in the first place. Most officers had affluent families in France and were allowed to receive money forwarded to them, which enabled them to live very well. They

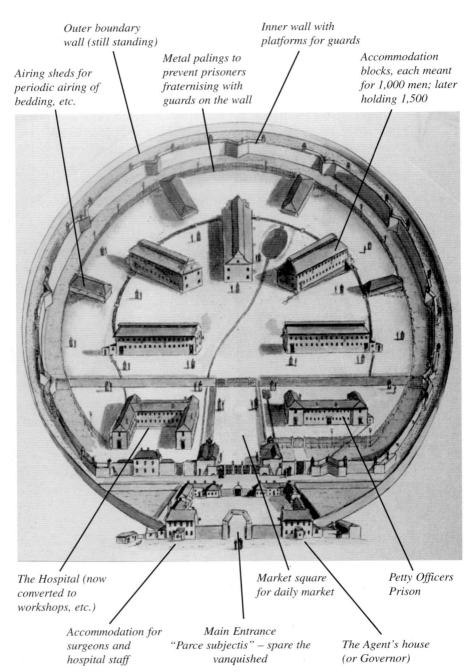

Outer boundary wall (still standing)

Inner wall with platforms for guards

Airing sheds for periodic airing of bedding, etc.

Metal palings to prevent prisoners fraternising with guards on the wall

Accommodation blocks, each meant for 1,000 men; later holding 1,500

The Hospital (now converted to workshops, etc.)

Market square for daily market

Petty Officers Prison

Accommodation for surgeons and hospital staff

Main Entrance "Parce subjectis" – spare the vanquished

The Agent's house (or Governor)

From a painting by Paul Deacon of an old Manuscript.

employed men and boys from the lower ranks to cook and wait on them, paying them a wage from their own pockets.

Close by the hospital was the dreaded 'Cachot' or 'Black Hole' as the British called it. It was a punishment cell, made entirely of stone blocks with a reinforced metal door, having an aperture through which rations could be passed. This was where men who were recaptured whilst trying to escape were put, and those who broke prison rules such as assaulting the guards or buying and selling other prisoner's rations. Corporal punishment was forbidden by mutual agreement with the enemy and the Black Hole was the only method of keeping order (the French too had their 'Cachots' for British prisoners). The maximum sentence was ten days, always on two thirds rations, with no bedding and in perpetual darkness, there being no window, only a small grill for ventilation. In winter men were often carried away to the hospital suffering from hypothermia.

Outside the prison, to the left of the main entrance, was the accommodation for the Medical and Administration staff. Opposite, to the right, was the home of the Agent and his family (today it is the Prison Officers Mess). The Agent or Governor was appointed by the Transport Office and was a Post Captain of the Royal Navy. The famous archway stands astride the entrance itself and has become a symbol of Dartmoor prison. The inscription overhead reads *'Parcere Subjectis'* (Spare the Vanquished), an appropriate greeting for prisoners taken in battle.

Dartmoor Prison courtyard looking out to main entrance and water tower.

PRISONER OF WAR

The first 250 French prisoners of war to be transferred from the hulks at Plymouth, marched to the prison on 24th May 1809. By the end of the year the prison was nearly full with more than 5,000 men within its grim walls. More than 460 Frenchmen died that winter from an outbreak of measles. By the time the French wars *finally* ended in 1815 (after the Battle of Waterloo) 1,250 had died, mostly from smallpox, typhus and chest complaints that often led to pneumonia. In 1813 American prisoners started arriving, captives taken in the War of 1812 and the overcrowding became almost intolerable. They suffered a total loss of 267 men, mainly from a smallpox epidemic which swept through their ranks during the winter of 1814/15, after the French had gone.* Altogether around 1500 men died on the moor between 1809 and 1815, mostly from disease. Some were killed by the guards whilst trying to escape, or murdered during quarrels among themselves, plus a few who died of exposure or malnutrition after gambling (and losing) their clothes or rations. Sadly, there were also some suicides. Those who died were buried outside the prison walls, either in cheap wooden coffins, or simply wrapped in a shroud, without mourners present or religious ceremony. More than fifty years later their bones littered the area, having been exposed by Dartmoor weather and the wild animals. In 1866 the Governor of the convict prison ordered them to be collected and divided into two heaps which were designated French or American remains. These were reverently interred in separate cemeteries at the rear of the prison. Over each mass grave a cairn was built, surmounted by an obelisk, suitably inscribed to identify which nationality it represented and the salutation: *'Dulce et Decorum est pro Patria Mori'* ('it is sweet and honourable to die for one's country').

From the beginning there was a daily market held within the walls, where farmers and traders came to sell or barter tobacco, coffee, poultry and other items to supplement the prisoner's allowance. Prisoners who did not have any money used their ingenuity to make trinkets and models to sell or exchange. These included beautiful objects of wood and bone, snuff boxes, delicate models of ships and all kinds of ornaments. Those that have survived are extremely valuable today and can be seen in museums all over Britain, but most of them are in private hands and will remain family heirlooms.

As the prison filled the lucky ones got jobs – the establishment needed barbers, cooks, sweepers, hospital helpers and so on. As already mentioned,

---

* See Notable Dates, page 30

they were paid a wage and as money began to circulate throughout the prison enterprising men set up market stalls of their own, selling tasty snacks made from ingredients bought at the regular market, clothes and even other prisoners' rations lost at gambling. In 1812 prisoners were employed as masons and labourers to build Princetown church, but the French war ended before the work was done, and the Americans completed the job. The church is unique in all of Britain, having been built by prisoners of war.

The rations were similar to those allocated to sailors of the Royal Navy and were certainly better than that of the labouring classes at that time. It was prepared in the 'cookeries' and served up as soup, to be collected by representatives for each mess of six men, together with a daily 9lb. loaf (1½lb. per man per day). It was not a generous allowance but at least the basic contents were fairly fresh, unlike the often dubious quality issued to British 'Tars' at sea.

Discipline within the prison was maintained by the prisoners themselves, who appointed leaders and committees to exercise an acceptable rule of law. The Americans not only elected their committees, but sent 'criers' through the prisons to announce their decisions, when the men would respond by shouting 'aye' or 'nay'. They punished those who broke the rules, often by a flogging with hammock cords. More serious offences were of course dealt with by the Agent.

Bone model made by a French prisoner of war. It is approximately 10 inches long – an indication of the intricate workmanship.
Reproduced courtesy of Mrs M. Hooper, Chagford.

It was a tough life, even for seasoned sailors, which most of them were in the early days (most of the soldier prisoners came later when the British began winning victories in the Peninsula). Life at sea was hard, but it was active and healthy, a far cry from being confined in a prison with comparatively little to do and because the majority of these men came from warmer climates, they suffered greatly from the cold, which must have contributed to the number of deaths.

The American memorial.

French and American Prisoners of War – Table of Daily Ration

Days	Bread	Beef	Codfish	Herrings	Potatoes	Greens	Scotch Barley	Onions	Salt
	lb.	lb.	lb.	lb.	lb.	lb.	oz.	oz.	oz.
Sunday	1.5	0.5	-	-	-	0.5	1.0	qtr	third
Monday	1.5	0.5	-	-	-	0.5	1.0	qtr	third
Tuesday	1.5	0.5	-	-	-	0.5	1.0	qtr	third
Wednesday	1.5	-	-	1.0	1.0	-	-	-	-
Thursday	1.5	0.5	-	-	-	0.5	1.0	qtr	third
Friday	1.5	-	1.0	-	1.0	-	-	-	-
Saturday	1.5	0.5	-	-	-	0.5	1.0	qtr	third
TOTAL	10.5	2.5	1.0	1.0	2.0	2.5	5.0	1¼	1²/₃

THE DEPOT'S LAST DAYS

When the war with France ended in April 1814 the French prisoners at Dartmoor were repatriated, and all American prisoners of war in Britain (except the officers on parole) were moved there to take their place, more than 5,000 of them. The British, who had been fighting two wars at the same time, could now concentrate all her forces against the United States, but by December that year both countries were glad to end hostilities and the Treaty of Ghent was signed, very appropriately on Christmas Eve. There was a long delay in arranging for the 'Yankees' to be repatriated and tension between them and the guards became intolerable. In April 1815, whilst waiting for transport to take them home, there was a violent demonstration when nine of them were killed and an unknown number wounded, after the Militia guards opened fire. The 'Princetown Massacre', as it came to be called, was a tragic episode, the dead and wounded being no longer prisoners of war but free men, and the 'Yankees' never forgave us for it. They began leaving for Plymouth to embark for America soon afterwards, the first ones to arrive at Dartmoor being the first to leave.

Meanwhile Napoleon, who had been allowed to live in exile on the Mediterranean island of Elba, returned to France in March 1815 and swept back to power. Thus began what was afterwards called the 'Hundred Days', during which Britain and her Allies joined forces and inflicted a last terrible defeat on the French at Waterloo. The prisoners taken were sent to Dartmoor and began arriving, some of them for a second time, as the Americans were still in the process of leaving. Not long afterwards Napoleon, who had surrendered to the British, was sent into exile to St. Helena. The remnants of his army were then released from Dartmoor and sent home, the last of them leaving the moor in February 1816. The Militia then went home and were disbanded, leaving the prison deserted and Princetown in decline.

Over the next thirty four years the Duchy maintained the prison blocks and the barracks, in the hope a use would be found for them. A number of suggestions were made, among them one by Prince Albert, Queen Victoria's Consort and a man of vision, who thought the place might be suitable for convicted criminals. In 1846 one of the prisons was leased to the British Patent Naphtha Company, who installed retorts for the production of gas and oils extracted from the Dartmoor peat, but operations ceased when it was found the quantity and quality of produce was unsatisfactory. In the end the Prince's idea was adopted and Dartmoor was made ready to receive convicted criminals.

THE CONVICTS

In 1850 the prison opened its gates again, as an establishment for criminals who could no longer be transported. The Colonies, which had long been used as a dumping ground for Britain's convicts, were now refusing to take any more and transportation ceased after 1853. Meanwhile the prisons and convict hulks were filling up, prompting the authorities to find another way of dealing with convicted men. It was decided to transfer as many of them as possible to prisons where they could be employed doing work similar to what they would have done overseas. Among those selected were: 1848 Portland (quarrying), 1850 Portsmouth (building the docks) and Dartmoor (quarrying and cultivating the moor).

Among the entrants to Dartmoor were invalids from the hospital prison at Woking (opened in 1859), who were expected to benefit from the fresh moorland air, among them men with chest complaints, others with crooked spines and a few weak minded individuals. Many men were sent from the hulks 'Garth' and 'Stirling Castle' at Gosport and the 'Warrior' and 'Defence' at Woolwich. After a time Dartmoor received the most vicious and incorrigible of men, banished it was hoped, to a remote area where they would be 'out of sight and out of mind'. One example was Joseph Crove who was transferred to Dartmoor from Pentonville in 1854. His conduct was stated to be *'thoroughly bad, having been punished 15 times and removed from the 'Warrior' hulk for violent and outrageous conduct for which corporal punishment and extended sentence had been awarded'* (from the Governor's journal 1854). By 1880 the worst convicts in the country ended up at Dartmoor, all of them with no less than five years to serve. Eighteen months solitary confinement (later reduced to twelve, then nine because men were going insane) preceded the transfer of offenders to Dartmoor (as well as other prisons) to commence their sentences. The idea was to 'break them in' to prison life, enable them to reflect on their crimes and do useful tasks such as picking oakum – lengths of tarred rope, hard as iron, had to be unpicked by hand – a difficult and painful task. The fibres were used to caulk the seams of wooden decks on ships. Added to this was the 'Silent Rule' which originated in the United States and was intended to discourage the 'old lags' from contaminating younger offenders. It meant precisely what the title implied – no talking, whispering, nodding of heads or attempting to communicate with another prisoner in any way. The rule of silence followed them to Dartmoor where the Warders rigidly enforced it, and were themselves liable for punishment for any infringements.

Convicts being escorted from the prison to work on the farm and quarry.

The first men to arrive (in November 1850) were artisan convicts who converted one of the old French prisons to single cell accommodation, a requirement for penal establishments. This was done by dismantling the concrete floors, and constructing tiers of corrugated iron cells, arranged back to back, with platforms between them and the walls for the guards to patrol. There the prisoners lived in perpetual gloom, with no ventilation other than a gap under each door, and a pot for a toilet which was emptied every morning ('night soil' they called it) into the tubs provided on each level. They slept in hammocks at first, then on wooden planks with two blankets and a coir pillow. The iron cells were the warmest, compared to the stone cells which replaced them afterwards and were always damp (sometimes the water that accumulated on the floor had to be mopped up several times a day). Eventually all but three of the old French prisons were demolished* to make way for the multi-storey granite prison blocks of today, all of which were built with convict labour and to the single cell design.

The renewed Duchy lease was conditional on the inmates being employed reclaiming the moor in order to drain it and make it suitable for cultivation.

---

* One is still in use after extensive modernisation. The other two are the 'Old Chapel' and what used to be the prison kitchen, both of them now redundant.

New arrivals to Dartmoor were examined by the Medical Officer, and those deemed fit were put to work, either in the prison quarry or on the land, the fortunate ones graduating to more amenable work in one of several workshops. Gangs of men dug the bogs by hand in line abreast, sometimes up to their knees in water; others learned the rudiments of quarrying granite (some of them were killed in accidents) and breaking rocks with hammers. Armed guards, some of them on horseback, kept a menacing vigil on outside working parties and several men were shot, often with fatal results whilst trying to run away.

It was a harsh regime, enforced by Warders who were mostly ex-servicemen or tough men recruited from the mines and quarries. Yet, even for such men as these, life was hard. In the early days many of them either resigned or asked to be transferred, on account of their own or their family's ill health. Their accommodation, almost as spartan as that of their charges, comprised stone built terraced houses, damp and dismal, with a peat hearth for warmth. The only respite was to be found in the pubs. At last the authorities provided a recreation hall and a school. The Church played its part organising social events, especially for the children, but the best thing that ever happened was the opening in 1883 of the Princetown branch of the old Great Western Railway, enabling wives and families to 'escape' occasionally to the shopping delights of Plymouth on the 'Princetown Flier', as the train was called. As late as the 1950s Warders from other prisons were drafted to Princetown to 'do their stint' because of staffing difficulties, mainly because it was compulsory for them to live there. Today there are no such restrictions and the majority of Prison Officers commute from Tavistock and the Plymouth area.

Dartmoor Prison warders outside the prison's main entrance during the Victorian era.
Reproduced courtesy of Mr R.G. Sandford

PUNISHMENTS

There was never a Treadmill at Dartmoor, they didn't need one - there was hard toil enough reclaiming the moor. Punishments ranged from a flogging with the cat o' nine tails or the birch rod, to three days solitary confinement on a diet of bread and water - the notorious 'jockey diet' (guaranteed to ensure a weight loss)*. The 'cat' was a whip with nine lashes or 'tails' and a short handle, and it often scarred a man for life, not only physically but in mind and spirit. A guard once told a troublesome inmate: *'Don't upset Warder W____, he's the hardest flogger in the prison – blood every time!'*. Yet it was the birch that was most feared, probably on account of the indignity imposed on the victim, who was thrashed on the bare buttocks and therefore could not boast to his mates how he had 'took his dozen like a man'. To administer a whipping, the victim was fastened by his wrists and ankles to a special 'flogging frame' (there is one on display in the Prison Museum). The same frame had a horizontal padded bar over which an offender was bent to receive a birching. Offences for which corporal punishment was inflicted were: trying to escape, inciting a mutiny and assaulting a Warder, which is probably why the biggest and strongest Officer available was often chosen for this gruesome task. In 1938 the Prison Rules and Orders stipulated the Officer who carried out a flogging was entitled to an extra payment of 2s.6d. (12½p).

There were occasions when frustrated prisoners went berserk (they still do) and wrecked their cells or perhaps tore up their clothes in protest. Canvas suits were issued in the latter case and the culprits made to wear them sometimes without underwear, even in winter. There were other men who did all they could to avoid work. An extreme example was a convict who refused to get up every morning for weeks, feigning an illness which the prison doctor was unable to identify. In the end the Governor ordered him to be carried to the prison quarry every day, where he was laid out on the ground until finishing time and then carried back to his cell. Not long afterwards he made a remarkable recovery, realising his efforts were futile.

There are numerous incidents on record where Warders were cut down and nearly killed by convicts wielding spades and other implements. Many of them were revenge attacks on unpopular men. There was undoubtedly a degree of bitterness on the part of some prisoners who either fell foul of a Warder or felt a keen sense of injustice they could do nothing about. In 1932 a convict

---

* In 1938 the diet consisted of one pound of bread per day with water – for a maximum of three days at a time.

who had escaped and been recaptured, was put in solitary confinement to await punishment. He had a serious chest infection (later diagnosed as pneumonia) as a result of falling into a river whilst 'on the run', which was why he'd been given an extra blanket. When the Governor visited him in his cell he asked if he could keep the extra blanket because it was so cold and when this was refused he hit out and struck the Governor to the ground. This merited thirty six lashes with the 'cat', to be administered when he recovered, but as he had been so ill the Home Secretary decided fourteen strokes with the birch rod would suffice. As soon as he was well enough he was taken from the hospital to receive his punishment. He was forty years of age and never made a sound. A concerned member of the medical staff went to see him in his cell and found him lying face down on his bed. The following conversation then took place.

M.O. 'Well Fred, what has this done for you?'

Victim 'You mean done *to* me don't you?'

M.O. 'Yes I suppose so, but would you do the same thing again?'

Victim 'Course I would. I got flogged before – that didn't stop me did it? I'll do a better job next time!'

M.O. 'Did you think you might get a reprieve because you were sick?'

Victim 'Course not. They'd have flogged my dead body'.

'I felt guilty and ashamed at being an accomplice to such a deed' was the M.O.'s comment. 'It was counter violence, which brought out nothing but the worst in all concerned'.

A recaptured prisoner today is dealt with by the Governor, who has the authority to award a loss of remission (in any case the time spent out of prison before recapture doesn't count towards the prisoner's original sentence). If an offence was committed whilst at large, he will be tried by the local magistrates and sentenced accordingly, any such sentence being added to the original.

No more mailbags! A modern textile shop. Dartmoor prison is changing.

ESCAPES

The sentries in the War Depot had no hesitation in shooting or bayoneting anyone attempting to escape. A soldier found assisting an escape was Court Martialled, and if guilty was flogged or executed. Despite this, several French and American prisoners of war did manage to bribe the guards, who either helped them over the walls or turned a blind eye at a crucial moment. Some men cultivated friendly relations with the market traders and obtained civilian clothes, mingling with them on their departure and making off. A few prisoners were able to 'borrow' a uniform (at a price of course) and simply walked out of the prison with the soldiers. The Americans tried digging their way out under the prison walls, not one tunnel but *three,* all at the same time. They were betrayed by one of their own number, thus preventing what would have been a mass escape.

If we include the French and American prisoners who escaped from Dartmoor, and officers who absconded whilst on parole, the total runs into hundreds. Convicts nearly always made their 'break' in the thick mists so prevalent on the moor and most often from an outside working party. A popular conception is of fugitives being pursued over Dartmoor by Officers with bloodhounds, and there were occasions when this happened – the police had an arrangement with a lady who bred them and a Constable was dispatched to collect one or two when there was an escape. In the old days the alarm was raised by a gunshot; then a warning bell took its place*, after which a siren was installed. Radio communication has superseded them all.

Boys like these were sent to Dartmoor from Parkhurst (Isle of Wight) in 1860. Two of them escaped and were never caught.
Reproduced courtesy of Hampshire County Council.

---

* *The bell can still be seen above the main prison entrance and was last rung as an escape warning in 1931.*

Throughout Dartmoor Prison's history every escapee has had to face the hazards on the moor, a vast expanse of barren heath and bogs and rocky tors. In winter the terrible cold can kill a man caught in the open without adequate clothing and many a convict has been glad to be apprehended after a soaking on Dartmoor, perhaps in biting winds and having had nothing hot to eat or drink. Among the earliest escapes (February 1853) was that of a man called Brown who ran off during a blizzard and lost his toes through frostbite after being recaptured. In 1860 a number of boy convicts were transferred to Dartmoor from the Isle of Wight, and two of them, both under twelve years of age, escaped over the walls with an older man and were not seen again. These were the days of the 'Broad Arrow', when convicts' hats and clothes were stamped with distinctive arrows (the War Department still use them to mark Government property), and nails were driven into the soles of their boots in the shape of an arrow, the idea being that wherever an escaped convict trod he would leave a trail. The first thing convicts did when they absconded was get rid of their boots before looking for a house to break into where they could steal plain clothing.

Dartmoor Prison's most notorious escapee was Frank Mitchell (the 'Mad Axeman'), who vanished from a group of prisoners at work several miles from the prison in December 1966, and was never recaptured*. Special mention should be made of John Charles 'Ruby' Sparks, who got away in January 1940 and was free for a total of 170 days, an all time record for Dartmoor. His background is interesting: he was dubbed 'Ruby' by the London underworld after breaking into a Park Lane apartment belonging to a Maharajah and stealing, among other things, a quantity of rubies which he gave away, believing them to be fakes. In fact they were worth over £40,000! In November 1951 'Rubber Bones' Webb wriggled to freedom after breaking into the warm air heating ducts under his cell and crawling through stifling hot fumes, in the dark, to the fresh air intakes. He was over the wall and making his way to the main railway line to London before he was found to be missing, having left a 'dummy' under the blankets in his cell. Because he managed to deceive the 'screws' so successfully, even though he was under constant observation as a previous escapee, he became an instant hero to his fellow prisoners. He just as quickly earned their contempt when he gave in without a struggle after being apprehended whilst sleeping under a barrow in a London cul-de-sac. Then there was 'Foxy' Fowler, who escaped in the fog in May 1957, one of the few men who got out of the County (the searchers met a party of huntsmen on the moor who abandoned their prey and joined in pursuit of Fowler, which it is said, is how

---

He was murdered whilst at large and his body was never found

he came to be dubbed 'Foxy'). He was recaptured in Cumberland after thirty three days on the run.

Every trick you ever heard of has been used by determined men breaking out from Dartmoor. Convicts have dug down through floors, prised stones out of their cell walls and even managed to hack their way through the barred windows, using makeshift ropes to lower themselves to the ground. Escapes are rare nowadays, mainly because every incident has always been thoroughly investigated and any 'loopholes' in security eliminated; but there are inmates who regard this as a challenge, have plenty of time to work out a new method of escape, and are watching for an opportunity to try it.

Princetown church with convict headstones and memorial cross.

MUTINY!

There are very few privileges in any prison and those they have are jealously guarded by the inmates. A common complaint is about the food, however plain the daily fare might be, simply because in the daily grind of prison life it is one of the few things a prisoner can look forward to. The incident when the Americans were fired upon in 1815 was linked to a serious confrontation the previous day over the quality of the bread. In 1932 the convicts rioted over the quality of their porridge. On Sunday 24th January of that year approximately 150 out of 440 inmates, all hardened criminals, ran amok after complaining for days about watered-down porridge for breakfast. The matter came to a head when the men were assembled for Sunday morning service. Upon a shouted signal they broke off in groups and proceeded to rampage through the prison, most of them engaging in a frenzy of destruction. Princetown residents heard a roaring from within the prison walls that scared them sick, especially those whose husbands were on duty. The Prison Officers, heavily outnumbered, were forced to retreat. Several other Officers who were trapped in the lower part of the prison, were attacked and injured.

The Governor and his Deputy were talking to Colonel Turner, a Home Office official on a visit, when they were alerted by the noise. Colonel Turner went out and tried to reason with the rioters only to be assaulted (he had a bowl of porridge tipped over him); he was saved from serious injury by a loyal convict who whisked him away to a cell and locked him in (he had only to slam the door). A howling mob, out to 'get the Governor', then smashed their way in through the office windows, upon which the Governor and Deputy Governor ran outside, slamming the door in their faces. They managed to get into one of the old French prisons where they hid for the duration of the mutiny. Shortly afterwards the Administration Block was set on fire. After burning all day it was completely gutted and all the prison records were destroyed with it. By this time the scene in the yards resembled a nightmare: men were screaming abuse, fighting among themselves over food and cigarettes they discovered, and some were blaring out tunes on instruments belonging to the prison band, whilst their mates partnered each other for clumsy 'dancing'. Other men were wandering aimlessly beneath the huge cloud of black smoke rising from the burning Administration building, unable to come to terms with their new-found 'freedom'. Weapons were sought and found – hammers from the internal stone sheds, butcher's knives taken from the kitchen, iron bars, wooden axe handles and any tools to hand. The convicts had complete control of the prison and were looking for anyone or anything to attack.

At the first sign of trouble a quick-thinking Officer at the gate had telephoned the police at Plymouth for help, and all available Prison Officers were issued with Snider rifles loaded with buckshot, before being posted around the perimeter. It was just as well, because when certain prisoners popped their heads over the wall (they had taken the ladders from the prison fire appliance), they dropped out of sight when they saw armed men surrounding the place. One inmate got on to the roof of a building near the gate and was shot and injured, leaving his colleagues in no doubt the authorities meant business.

'As big as a Stonehouse copper' the saying went, because they all had to be six foot tall or more, and they were among the Plymouth policemen who were sent to sort out the trouble at Princetown that day. Soldiers from the 8th Infantry Brigade at Crownhill Barracks also attended, but their services were not required. The Police tried to negotiate a peaceful surrender with the mutineers, but were greeted with jeers of derision, whereupon they drew their 'sticks' (truncheons) and charged into the prison yard – about 30 police and a handful of Prison Officers against 100 or so convicts. It was all over in minutes, and the now subdued culprits were led away to be locked up. *These chaps are pretty tough when menacing the weak and defenceless*' remarked one policeman, *'but you should hear the squeals when they are on the receiving end'.*

Aftermath:

Thirty-one mutineers were tried at a temporary court set up in Princetown and extra sentences were awarded to the ringleaders. During the mutiny no-one escaped and, miraculously, no-one was killed, but there was a queue of inmates outside the prison hospital that day for treatment to broken limbs and one fractured skull.

There was another serious outbreak in 1990, not only at Dartmoor but at several prisons nationwide. A prison block at Dartmoor was wrecked beyond recognition and some prisoners got on the roof, shouting their grievances (real and imagined) to anyone who would listen. Tragically one inmate died. The pile of wreckage they left when it was finally over was astounding – beds, mattresses, chairs and tables, personal possessions, utensils, lockers, even broken off handrails, lay in an enormous heap on the ground floor. The cost was estimated to be in excess of £500,000.

CONVICT LIFE.

By 1880 there was a variety of employment in the convict prison. The quarry and the reclaiming of the moor have already been mentioned. In addition there was a tailor's shop where uniforms were made for the Prison Service and the Metropolitan Police, and a shoemaking shop making them boots. The carpenter shop made doors and replacement windows for the Warders' accommodation, and the smithy manufactured metal posts, gates, wheels etc. for the prison and farm. All the work was done by convicts under supervision. Employment on the prison farm was eagerly sought after by inmates, many of whom came from the towns and had never seen a live sheep or cow before. They were allowed to keep the field mice they caught as pets and the little creatures were taught tricks, accompanying their owners everywhere (they kept them inside their shirts in case someone tried to steal them). A legendary figure was a Welshman called David Davies, a compulsive church offertory box robber and a frequent 'guest' at Dartmoor, remembered today as the 'Prison Shepherd'. He knew every sheep in his charge and was able to call them to him by name, a phenomenon that was witnessed by Mr. David Lloyd George who visited the prison and conversed with him in Welsh (he was instrumental in gaining Davies an early release, but it wasn't long before the 'Shepherd' was back at Dartmoor with his flock). The farm also kept pigs, cattle and horses, winning many prizes at local shows and bringing an additional income to the prison. The farm fields, created from the virgin moor, all have names associated either with certain people or their proximity to known landmarks. Hence there are Fices Well Field, Bridge Field, Rocky Field and Conchie Field. The last named was established when over 1,000 'Conscientious Objectors' were admitted to Dartmoor prison in 1917, the convicts being moved elsewhere.

Both Naval Surgeons in the War Depot days, and more than one Medical Officer of the convict era, have recorded their opinion that Dartmoor is a fine healthy location. The sight of fit and bronzed men marching briskly to and from the outside working parties has been mentioned by several observers, including ex-convicts who afterwards wrote about their experiences. The majority of deaths on the Moor have either been the result of diseases brought about by overcrowding, as in the case of the French and American P.O.W.s, or in the convicts' case, dietary complaints – dropsy and dysentery for example, in addition to periodic outbreaks of typhus, one of cholera and a great many who died during the influenza epidemic after World War 1.

In 1871 a typical daily ration would have been:

6.00 a.m. Breakfast: gruel (watery porridge) and bread.

11.30 a.m. Dinner: boiled meat or suet pudding or soup, with potatoes and bread.

6.00 p.m. Supper: cocoa and bread.

Note the absence of green vegetables or fruit (the French prisoners of war fared better sixty years before). Today's inmates have an approved diet, with the quantity of vegetables, etc. needed to sustain good health, and special menus are provided for vegans, vegetarians, Muslims, Jews and the men who are sick.

The convicts rose at 5.30 a.m., 'lights out' was at 8.00 p.m., and they were not permitted to lie on their beds within these times. There was a compulsory church parade every day at 7.00 a.m. when a harmonium accompanied a thirty strong choir to lead the hymn singing. Only members of the Church of England, Roman Catholics and Jews were recognised then. Today all other Christian denominations are catered for and there is a 'Multi-Faith' room reserved for other religions. In the restricted free time, some evening classes were available in a variety of subjects, including English, and there was a library. To get a library book a man asked for the subject or title he wanted to read and (if he was lucky) it was handed to him in his cell. One convict asked for what he called 'Less Miserable' because he thought it might cheer him up! These days an inmate can have any book or periodical he wants sent in (provided he can pay for it), as well as the use of the prison library.

Inmates used to bathe once a week in a communal bath house and this continued to be the rule until beyond 1990, when a refurbishing programme began to install showers in every block with no restrictions on their use.

Going to Princetown to see the 'Transports' was a popular diversion up until the late 1870s when visitors were shown over the prison and notable inmates were pointed out. There have been several well known prisoners at Dartmoor, among whom were:

Michael Davitt, Fenian sympathiser and founder of the Irish Land League.

George Bidwell who with an accomplice tricked the Bank of England out of an enormous sum of money.

Eamonn de Valera, Irish 'rebel', later to become the first Prime Minister of the Republic of Ireland.

John George Haigh, dubbed the 'Acid Bath' murderer. Sent to the Moor convicted of fraud, before committing the grisly crimes for which he was later executed.

James Camb who murdered an actress on board a Union Castle liner and dumped her body overboard. He was sentenced to be hanged, but was reprieved when capital punishment was suspended prior to being abolished.

Frank Mitchell, the 'Mad Axeman' (he never killed anyone by the way), whose escape caused the biggest manhunt ever mounted on Dartmoor and resulted in the complete overhaul of the prison's security system.

Stephen Downing served 27 years in various prisons after being wrongfully convicted of murdering a woman in Bakewell, Derbyshire.

Some of these offenders are forgotten today, but their crimes made newspaper headlines all over the world. There have also been men at Dartmoor whose records are so abominable and shocking the author prefers not to record their names or details of the loathsome crimes for which they were convicted.

Convicts taking shelter on the moor, c.1870s.
Reproduced courtesy of Dartmoor Prison Museum.

IS THERE A GHOST AT DARTMOOR PRISON?

Over a hundred years ago a convict working in the American Cemetery had a strange experience, not the only one of its kind. The cemetery at the rear of the prison contains the bones of those French and American prisoners of war who died in captivity at Dartmoor during the Napoleonic Wars and the War of 1812. They lie in separate mass graves, each of which is surmounted by a memorial stone in the form of an obelisk with an inscription commemorating their deaths. 'Jock of Parkhurst' was the name under which a former British Army officer, who went astray and served part of his sentence on the 'moor,' wrote about his life in prison. This is how he described what happened:

'I myself was employed in the American graveyard for several weeks, cutting the grass and weeding the paths. One day I saw an old grey-haired lady – a very old lady she seemed – kneeling before the stone. I looked round for the officer, thinking he might speak to her. He was outside on the road. I went to tell him and he came back with me, but the old lady had gone. We looked in every direction. Then he recommended me to report sick when we returned to the prison. I went back to the stone, and there on the ground we saw a bunch of red roses – roses but freshly cut. I wonder if anyone else has ever seen the Old Lady of the American Graveyard.'

There have been other sightings of figures, imaginary or by honest mistake, over the years. In a place like Dartmoor Prison with its long history, where sad and often macabre events have occurred, it is perhaps what you would expect. However, this event occurred in daylight, in the open and a long way off the public highway. An old lady would not be capable of making off so quickly as not to be seen and the writer was certainly sober and necessarily of sound mind to have placed on record what he experienced in such lucid terms. The mystery remains.

CLOSING COMMENTS

When Dartmoor was a war prison it was badly overcrowded and there were periodic outbreaks of diseases that killed hundreds at a time, giving the place a fearsome reputation. A 'trip over the Alps' as it was known, was equally feared by the convicts and Warders who arrived at a later date. A lurid fascination with Dartmoor Prison endures to this day and is reflected in the number of people who come to Princetown each year just to see the place. It goes further. There have been instances where inmates did not want to be transferred to another prison because they cannot bear to go home after release and admit to not having served their time in 'a tough jail'. There are other inmates who will admit Dartmoor is not such a bad place after all. The main drawback is, and has always been, the remote location, which makes it difficult for visitors to attend.

Inmates (no longer referred to as 'convicts') now live in a vastly different environment to that of their predecessors and enjoy the benefit of central heating, a balanced diet and telephone contact with their families. It is now recognised men are sent to prison as a punishment – not to receive it, and this is summed up by the Prison Service reminder, prominently displayed in every prison:

'HER MAJESTY'S PRISON SERVICE PROTECTS THE PUBLIC BY KEEPING IN CUSTODY THOSE COMMITTED BY THE COURTS. OUR DUTY IS TO LOOK AFTER THEM WITH HUMANITY AND TO HELP THEM LIVE LAW ABIDING AND USEFUL LIVES IN CUSTODY AND AFTER RELEASE'.

Most people do not know there are several women Officers at Dartmoor, doing exactly the same job as their male colleagues. The Prison Officer of today is as unlike the Warder of long ago as a Policeman is to a 'Bow Street Runner' but the same cannot always be said of prisoners. The same old tricks are tried by inmates trying to beat the system, but the training and periodic refresher courses keep Officers abreast of the latest developments. In any case most of them are ex-servicemen who have 'seen it all before' – or have they? Not long ago, on the day of his release, a prisoner walked free from the jail and stepped into a chauffeur-driven Rolls Royce, upon which one Officer remarked (with a weary sigh): *'And they say crime doesn't pay!'*

Will Dartmoor close? It was first contemplated in the 1860s and in 1891 the *Western Morning News* (Plymouth) reported closure was imminent because the cost of running a prison in such a remote area was becoming prohibitive.

Well the prison is still there, despite more recent representations to government to shut it down. The fact is there are not enough prisons.

In May 2001 it was officially announced Dartmoor Prison will be regraded to provide safe custody for Category 'C' prisoners only (these are men who are not considered a high escape or security risk to the public). All Category 'B' inmates (men convicted of murder and other violent offences) will transfer to other establishments and with them will go the last vestige of a by-gone era when the moorland gaol confined the worst offenders in the worst of conditions. All that has long since been a thing of the past and Dartmoor Prison's inmates now live in modern conditions undreamed of by the convicts of old. However, life in prison is not a 'soft option' – loss of liberty has a devastating effect on some men. Dartmoor still provides single cell accommodation only, so the prisoners live alone outside working hours and the 'association' periods. They even take their meals alone in their cells. A notable Irish patriot (Michael Davitt), who was imprisoned at Dartmoor more than 100 years ago, wrote: *'Freedom is more to be desired than fetters of gold'* – a sentiment that was echoed by a present day inmate, when he was asked by the author how he liked his new cell in one of the refurbished prison blocks: *'I ain't too bothered, mate'* he replied, *'I'm just waiting to get out!'* .

The new kitchen building at Dartmoor Prison. 1994.

'LINES ON A GRAVESTONE AT DARTMOOR'.
By Robert Dymond.

Beneath this plain and silent stone,
Which hath no name engraved thereon –
No words of Holy Writ, to tell
To passers by what here befell –
The convict's worn and ragged form
Lies sheltered from life's bitter storm.
That storm of sin and misery,
Now hushed, hath set the prisoner free.
No other sickness shook his frame
But anguish for his tainted name:
He drooped whene're he thought upon
His distant wife, his helpless son.
What though his frailties dreadful were,
His punishment was hard to bear;
Cut off, like Cain, from every tie
That sweetens life, 'twas bliss to die.
Cast no uncharitable stone
At him, as if he sinned alone;
But weep a brother's fate; for grace
Alone hath saved *thee* from his place.

Princetown churchyard. The sad bleak rows of convict headstones with initials and date of death.

GOVERNORS OF DARTMOOR PRISON

CAPT. COTGRAVE R.N. 1809–1812
CAPT. SHORTLAND R.N. 1812–1816
CLOSED 1816–1850
CAPT. M. GAMBIER R.N. 1850–1854
W. MORRISH. 1854–1864
CAPT. G. CLIFTON 1864–1866
CAPT. W. P. STOPFORD 1866–1868
W. PITT-BUTTS 1868–1869
MAJ. F. H. NOOTT. 1869–1874
CAPT. W. V. F. HARRIS 1876–1879
CAPT. O. W. EVERY 1880–1890
NO RECORD. 1891–1892
CAPT. F. JOHNSON 1893–1899
W. H. O. RUSSELL 1900–1902
B. THOMSON. 1903–1907
CAPT. G. H. GUYON 1908–1910
CAPT. G. E. TEMPLE 1911–1913
MAJ. E. R. READE 1914–1919
MAJ. T. F. H. WISDEN 1920–1921
MAJ. F. G. C. M. MORGAN 1922–1928
MAJ. G. F. CLAYTON. 1929–1930
MAJ. L. H. MORRIS M.C., L.L.D. 1930–1931
S. J. ROBERTS 1931–1932
MAJ. C. PANNALL O.B.E., M.C., D.S.O. 1932–1945
MAJ. HARVEY 1945–1955
J. RICHARDS 1955–1957
G. B. SMITH 1957–1960
D. G. W. MALONE 1960–1966
P. C. JONES 1966–1968
MAJ. N. A. GOLDING 1968–1974
G. B. HEALD 1974–1981
E. R. E. SKELTON 1981–1982
D. THOMSON 1982–1985
R. J. MAY 1985–1990
R. KENDRICK 1990–1992
J. POWLS 1992–1994
J. LAWRENCE 1994–2001
G. JOHNSON 2001–

NOTABLE DATES IN THE HISTORY OF DARTMOOR PRISON

1785	Sir Thomas Tyrwhitt leases land from the Duchy of Cornwall to farm on Dartmoor.
18 May 1803	War resumed with France. Old war prisons filled.
20 March 1806	Sir Thomas lays foundation stone for Dartmoor Prison of War.
24 May 1809	First French prisoners of war arrive from the Plymouth hulks.
18 June 1812	American War of 1812 commences.
3 April 1813	First American prisoners arrive from the Plymouth hulks.
30 April 1814	French war ends. Prisoners repatriated and all American prisoners in England transferred to Dartmoor.
24 December 1814	Treaty of Ghent ends the War of 1812.
26 February 1815	Napoleon returns to France and the 'Hundred Days' begins.
16 March 1815	News of the Ratification of the Treaty of Ghent reaches Princetown. Americans impatient for release.
6 April 1815	Militia guards open fire on unruly Americans. The 'Princetown Massacre'.
19 April 1815	First batch of Americans leave for home.
18 June 1815	Battle of Waterloo. Napoleon defeated.
1 July 1815	French prisoners arrive at Dartmoor straight from the battlefields, some for a second time.
24 July 1815	Last Americans depart. The war with France has ended.
16 February 1816	All prisoners of war have left and the Militia have gone home. Dartmoor prison closes.
November 1850	Dartmoor converted to a Penal Prison.
1853	Penal Servitude Act ends Transportation.
1914	Outbreak of World War 1.
1917	Convicts transferred and Dartmoor receives over 1,000 'Conscientious Objectors'.
January 1932	Dartmoor Prison mutiny. Army and Police called to restore order.
September 1939	Outbreak of World War II. Some military prisoners and IRA at Dartmoor.
1945	World War II ends. 'Borstal Boys' at Dartmoor.
1990	Riots. Prison block extensively damaged.
1994	Complete refurbishment programme in progress.
2001	Dartmoor Prison regraded Category 'C'.

Other Dartmoor Prison titles by Trevor James for Orchard Publications:

'There's One Away' – Escapes from Dartmoor Prison   P/back £3.95

Prisoners of War in Dartmoor Towns – French and American Officers on Parole 1803–1815   P/back £3.95